A Different Way Of Selling That Dares To Be Different

A Different Way Of Selling That Dares To Be Different

Barbara Hamilton

© 2018 Barbara Hamilton
All rights reserved.

ISBN: 1979380325
ISBN 13: 9781979380324

Contents

Introduction ································· vii

Is Your Pitch 'Out Dated' ························ 1
Are You In A Rut ······························ 6
The Dreaded Slump ···························· 11
Solutions For The Slump ······················· 16
A Dare To Be Different Salesperson ············· 20
Before Moving On ···························· 31
Reacting ····································· 32
Responding ·································· 35
Handling The ······························· 38
Dictionary Meanings For No ···················· 40
Personalities ································· 50
The Four Personalities ························ 52
Knowing Customer Concerns ··················· 60
Customer Concerns Samples ··················· 61
How To Design Selling Show Presentations ········ 67

Act 1 The Different Approach · 77
Example Of The Different Approach · · · · · · · · · · · · · · · · 85
Act 2 The Desk Show · 87
Act 3 Visual Show Of Benefits · 91
Ending Of Selling Show · 98
A Few Recaps · 101
Recap 1 The Gentle Art Of Persuasion · · · · · · · · · · · · · 103
Recap 2 Questions To Handle · · · · · · · · · · · · · · · · · · · 114
Recap 3 A Dare To Be Different Salesperson Is · · · · · · · 115
Recap 4 A Dare To Be Different Salesperson · · · · · · · · 117
Recap 5 A Dare To Be Different Salesperson · · · · · · · · 118
Are You Willing · 119
It Will Come To The Dare To Be Different Kind
Of Salesperson · 120

Introduction

So what really made me want to write this book, is because I know how I felt every time I went to buy something and all the sales people basically had the same greeting, 'Hi, can I help you,' and then follow me while I was looking. Boring. It finally got to the point where I began to do my best to avoid the sales people when shopping for anything.

I will start with a little of how and why I became a well known Top Sales Person and stayed that way for over a twenty five year career. First, I never liked doing what everyone else did, no matter what field I was in and so when I became a Salesperson I knew I had to do something that would make me really 'different' from other salespeople. I did not want to bore a customer, I wanted them to want to stay with me, so, I came up with a Different Kind Of Selling.

I do believe it was because I did Dare To Be Different in my Meet and Greet. and Different all through my Sales Presentation by using a Different Kind Of Selling Show Presentation, that I was chosen as one of the top three Coldwell Banker Real Estate Sales Agents in the state of California.

From there I went into the selling of Timeshares after I found out I could make the same kind of money in Timeshares that I did in general Real Estate, if not more, all without having to hunt for customers. I then spent a year with Lawerence Welk Timeshare Resorts and was Agent Of The Year, then they sold out and I went to Marriott Vacation Ownership near me, and was hired.

After I was hired and finished their training and was to go on the floor, I asked my Boss if I could please sell my own way. I was told NO. At that point I asked him if he would let me try selling my way for thirty days and if I didn't sell, he could fire me, or I would then do it his way. Well, he let me try my way and the rest is history.

I was one of the top sales agents for Marriott for Ten Years Straight. I also was one of, if not the first Marriott Vacation Ownership Sales Agent of Vacation Ownership to be honored into the Marriott's Presidential Club. When the Marriott where I worked sold out, I went to the Westin and was Top Agent my first year there. At that point my interest went to writing screenplays and reality shows, and being a top sales agent no longer mattered.

A Different Way Of Selling That Dares To Be Different

This book is from my own personal twenty five years of successful selling and staying at the top all those years. Now, understand I am 'not' a professional writer as you will see as you read on, and yes, I could have paid to have a professional writer or one to help write this book for me, but then it would not be mine alone. So I didn't.

I now no longer work, as I made enough money to purchase few Real Estate Investments, so now I totally spend most of my time in the pursuit of trying to understand, Metaphysics, Consciousness and Human Reality, and how they relate to ME.

Oh, this book is entirely 'different' than other selling books. It is a short read and it is extremely easy to understand. No long drawn out stuff. So I hope you get something from it.

Is Your Pitch 'Out Dated'

Before we move on it is important to know if your pitch, your sales presentation is designed for today's customers. Is yours? It might be good to ask yourself some questions, questions like, how long have you been giving your pitch? Is it the same one you gave years ago? Think now, how long have you been doing your sales pitch?

Another question is, do you think your pitch is cool? What makes it cool, if you think it is? And what do your customers think of your pitch? Do your customers also think it's cool? Do they seem interested in what you are saying? Or maybe you have not taken the time to notice if they seem interested or not. Have you ever taken the time to notice how interested a customer is, or are you so busy doing the pitch; you haven't noticed how they are taking it? What is it about your pitch that you think is cool and different? Do you think it fits today's customers? Do you? If so, why? What makes your sales pitch one customers would like?

Think now, what is it that is cool, modern and different about your sales pitch? How is it different from other sales pitches? Have you ever watched your pitch? Listened to your pitch, all the way though? Really think now, could it be possible, even a little, you could be bored doing your pitch? If you are, then how do you think your customers might feel?

Now ask yourself, at your first meeting with a customer, do you greet them the same way all other salespeople greet a customer? Or do you start out your pitch the same way every other salesperson starts off? Do you? If you do, your customer will instantly shut off their mind. They have heard and seen the same greeting and sales pitch for years. You should know, you do bore them if you are like the others.

Think now, if your customer is bored, they are most likely thinking, 'Oh no, let's get this over with.' Have you ever felt that way with a salesperson you were with? I promise you, this will not happen if you are not boring. So again, could you be bored doing your pitch? Really, might you be? Do you even care to find out if your sales pitch is outdated? If so, keep reading.

There is no reason for a boring, outdated salesperson, or a boring out dated sales pitch, and especially no reason for a bored customer. Again, take a minute and think, could you, are you bored giving your pitch. Be honest, are you?

A Different Way Of Selling That Dares To Be Different

To repeat, there is no reason for a boring salesperson or a bored customer or a boring out dated sales pitch. Just remember, your customers are bored with all sales presentation, no matter what one sells. They have seen and heard them all.

Another thing to ask yourself is, how many different pitches do you have? Do you have more than one, or do you use the same sales pitch with all your customers? So, how many pitches do you have?

And why is this an important question? How about this, a singer has more than one song. A dancer more than one dance. A restaurant more than one food. A car more than one model, ect. ect. Yes, it is necessary to have more than one pitch.

The reason a salesperson must have more than one way to present their product is because there are many types of customers and the salesperson should understand that customers are different, and one sales pitch cannot and will not work with all the different kinds of customers and their different personalities.

That means, if you only have one pitch, you are missing a lot of sales. I mean a lot of sales. So, that alone is a very good reason to have more than one sales pitch. Pitch? What a horrible word for a sales presentation, but we will get into that as you read on, so for now I will be using the word 'pitch.'

To repeat because it is really important to know. Have you ever noticed that your customers seem a little bored? A little not interested in what you are saying? Again, have you taken the time to notice if your customers seems bored as you do your sales pitch? You should, because a bored customer tells you they most likely will not purchase your product of service.

It is important to take some time and notice how your customers are reacting to you and your pitch, for if they do seem bored and not interested, that could be telling you it is now time for you to change your outdated sales pitch?

But you might think, oh no, no, I like my pitch, and because everyone knows change is hard, and change takes time, so no you think, my pitch is pretty good and I'll leave it alone. Sorry to tell you, but change you must if you want to step up your selling game for today's modern customers.

So just in case you do agree your pitch is outdated, and if you truly want to change your outdated, boring sales presentation, the first thing you need to do is to let go of your clinging to your old out dated habit of outdated selling. You will need to create and design a new kind of selling presentation for the new kind of customer of today.

That also means that you also must change and become a Dare To Be Different Salesperson for this new kind of customer. Yes, it will take some time and will take much creativity on your part in order for you to come up with Different Kind Of Selling Show Presentations. This small book is all about showing you how.

A Different Way Of Selling That Dares To Be Different

With all that said, unless you are at the top, maybe your pitch is outdated. Maybe you are bored with giving it, and maybe your customers are also bored with it also. So once again, could your sales pitch be outdated? It is easy to know, and how you know is, if you are in a 'rut.'

Are You In A Rut

The rut is that time when you are not selling and thinking maybe you may never sell again. Ruts are terrible and the longer they last, the harder to get out of. This Different Kind Of Selling Book will teach you how 'not' to get into ruts and how to get out quickly if you fall into one.

So, you're not selling and you have no idea how to get out of the 'rut' you find yourself in. You've thought of everything, but nothing helps. Well if nothing has worked, once again ask yourself, are you are 'bored' doing your same old sales pitch? And again, if you should feel 'bored' with your sales pitch, how do you think your customers feel? Maybe bored also and that's why they are not buying.

Do you understand what a 'rut' really is? Since Dare To Be Different salespeople always use a dictionary to help them better understand words and their meanings, that's what we will now do. Using a dictionary let's see what we can find for the

A Different Way Of Selling That Dares To Be Different

word, 'rut,' for knowing better what a 'rut' is, can then be used not to get into one and or, if in one how to quickly get out.

So looking at a meaning for the word 'rut,' we find a meaning of 'a established way of doing something.' Very interesting, 'an established way of doing something.' Is your way of selling 'an established way ' that you have used for years with all your customers? I mean, really, think about your sales pitch, is it the same one you have used for years? Is it, an established outdate pitch? Well it is, if it is the same one you have been doing for years. Period.

Another meaning for 'rut,' is 'fixed,' and a meaning for fixed is, 'stiff.' One meaning for 'stiff' is, 'difficult to accept in its severity and harshness.' Wow. So is it possible, you and your pitch are too severe? And if a meaning for 'severe' is, 'serious,' and you're in a 'rut,' then maybe, just maybe your sales pitch is too 'serious,' and that is why it is boring you and your customers. Think about that for a minute.

The word 'rut' also means, 'dull.' One meaning for dull is, 'causing boredom,' Rut means 'boredom? Again, wow. Do you find it interesting that one reason a salesperson gets into a rut is because they are bored doing their sales pitch? And they are in a 'rut' because their customers are also bored listening to it?

Another meaning for 'dull' is, 'uninteresting.' Do you find the way you are selling, is dull and uninteresting? Does it seem like your sales pitch causes boredom in your clients? Do they appear uninterested?

It might help you if you noticed them as it will tell if they are bored and uninterested. Yes, try watching your customers to see if they are uninterested in what you are saying. You might be surprised.

Another dictionary meaning for the word rut is a 'dreary routine.' Knowing that is a meaning for the word, are you in a rut? Close your eyes and think, are you dreary of your maybe too serious sales pitch? Then think, is your pitch just a routine, the routine of giving the same old outdated sales pitch?

And another dictionary meaning for the word 'rut,' is, 'habit.' A meaning for the word habit is, 'an acquired behavior regularly followed until it has become almost involuntary.' Is your sales pitch involuntary? Does it just kind of flows out without much thinking on your part?

Again think about that, do you think of your sales pitch as you are giving it, or does it just kind of 'routinely' comes out? If your sales pitch just comes out without much thought, then yes, you are in a habit, and a bad habit. So let's look at meaning for the word 'habit,' and see what we find.

Habit is a 'mental character,' and character, means, a 'role.' A meaning for 'role' is, 'expected behavior.' Expected, behavior? Another, wow.

Is that how you do your sales pitch, as the customer expects you too? Maybe that's a problem as you will find out

A Different Way Of Selling That Dares To Be Different

later. Remember, this book is about being 'different,' and you will get a good overview of your 'role' in the following chapters.

Once again, if your pitch just flows out of you, then yes, you may be in the habit of the dreary routine of giving the same old pitch? So think, have you fallen into a rut, a habit? You have if you are in the habit of doing the same sales pitch day after day. The same one that you did years ago?

If so, you in a rut? You do have a habit. If you do have the habit of giving the same sales pitch to each customer, then could it, is it now time for you to change? Wouldn't you like to do away with your habit of your clinging to an old outdated way of selling that bores you and your customers?

Looking at another meaning for the word 'habit,' we find 'doing the same thing.' Yep, another, wow. Again, are you, do you give the same sales pitch that you gave years ago? Most likely you do, and are. But why? Have not you changed other things over the years?

Things like your, Attire? Home? Car? Job? Restaurants? Girlfriends? Boyfriends? Or any number of things. I know I have. Well maybe it's time you do change your old selling habits, and to create a new Different Kind Of Selling Presentation, and the best way to do so, is to create Visual Selling Show Presentations, one's that fits today's customers. More on Visual Selling later on.

So instead of allowing yourself to continue the same old habit of 'sales pitching' the same old way, simply stop. I repeat it is only a habit, and yes, it is very hard to reprogram one's self, but the good news is, you can, and by you doing so, you are now in a 'different' frame of mind, and you can now start a new habit. How?

How about the habit of staying with the times. Yep, maybe it's time you become the deciding factor in how you do your sales presentation. Or, do you want the same outcome you have been having? Maybe it is time for you to let go of old habits? Old out dated ways to sell? So is it time to change, absolutely yes, it is time to change.

Yes, it might be good to change old habits, for it is truly a combination of habit and laziness that is keeping a salesperson from being the best. So if you are not at the top, wouldn't you like to be?

It's hard to admit that time honored ways of doing things might not be that effective with the changing world, so if you are in a rut, the habit of doing things like you always have, then it's time for you to change.

Again, you will find hange is not easy to accept, but change you must if you want to step up your selling abilities and get out of your rut, because by being in a rut, the habit of how you are currently selling, leads only to one thing.

 # The Dreaded Slump

You make no money when you hit a sales slump and you feel the pressure of your bosses on you, and your ego becomes unsure of ever selling again. So the question is, why do sales people who are not selling and find themselves in a rut, continue to keep doing the same sales pitch over and over?

Answer, its because of habit. Remember. And what happens other than not selling when you are in a slump? You become worried. You worry if you will ever sell again. You worry how you can pay your bills. You worry if you will keep your job, just to name a few worrisome things.

You also become fearful. Being fearful will really keep you from doing a 100% sales presentation. A part of your mind will be focused on all the worrisome things that are causing you not to be able to sell.

Being in the dreaded slump will cause irritability. The slump will cause you to do lots of complaining. The slump will also cause much disappointment.

It seems in most cases the customer is blamed, as that is the easiest, but the real cause is the salesperson. It is sad, but no salesperson wants to admit it, so they justify their lack of success on everything but themselves. But all along, it is the out dated boring sales pitch that is not working, and that is why no one is buying, and that is how they find themselves in the dreaded slump.

The Dare To Be Different Kind Of Salesperson would never blame anyone or anything on their not selling, knowing it is only them missing or leaving something out of their Different Kind Of Selling Show. By becoming a Dare To Be Different Salesperson, in most cases you would not find yourselves in a slump.

But, if you did, you would, should get a dictionary and investigate the word, slump. I cannot stress enough how important using a dictionary is, for in most cases knowing word meanings tell you just what to do or not do in and for you selling. Doing so, this is some of what of what you could find.

A Different Way Of Selling That Dares To Be Different

(According To Webster's Dictionary)

Slump: proceeding unevenly

What does proceeding unevenly mean? It means you must be jumping around during your sales pitch. It tells you, you are not presenting in a smooth and flowing manner.

These things should tell you, you have no plan, or if you do, you're not following it. Your sales pitch must flow from point to point, and the best way for that to happen is for you to create a Different Kind Of Sales Presentation that does flow easily. Again, more on this later.

Slump: not planned

If you have no plan, how can you get somewhere? If you have no plan, how do you know if you've covered all the important points? Without covering all the important points, you will not get a sale and you will be on your way to a slump.

Slump: laboriously

Laboriously means 'working too hard.' If you're working too hard then you are doing something wrong. You need to go back over your 'pitch' or your sales presentation to find the parts that are not flowing smoothly.

Slump: wilted

Wilted means 'dragging, dead or almost dead.' Having a wilted or dragging sales pitch only helps the client to drift off into their own thoughts, causing them not to hear you, and if they do not hear you, they will not buy, and if they do not buy, it means no sale. Which is how one gets into a slump.

Slump: lacking energy

So what does lacking energy mean in the sales pitch? No energy means your sales pitch is dying or is already dead. Without great energy, nothing lives. And certainly not a sales pitch. A meaning for 'energy' is, 'the ability to act, lead others.'

That is a good reason for any salesperson to want to be sure they and their selling has lots of 'energy,' if in fact they want to lead customers to the sale.

A sales pitch with no energy usually does not result in a sale, and no sale means you're heading for a slump. It is the Dare To Be Different Salesperson who has energy and is able to lead their customers to the 'yes' at the end.

Now something else to think about, and that is, sometimes when all is going our way and we are selling almost everyone we talk too we can get over confident and we may think its okay to take shortcuts.

A Different Way Of Selling That Dares To Be Different

It is never a good thing to take any shortcuts because shortcuts in the selling presentation will most likely end up costing you a lot of money, and shortcuts always end up causing you to go into a slump.

Just because you've been doing well doesn't mean you can get slack and do a 50% presentation. It takes you giving at least a 100% every time you do your sales presentation in order to stay good at it. So the slump is something, 'limp-laboriously-wilted-not planned and has no energy.' These are the main causes of a sales slump.

Sad, but this dreaded slump affects most parts of our work life and even some of our private life. But fear not, there are some things to do to help one get out of the dreaded slump.

Solutions For The Slump

First, take a long, deep breath. Second, stop looking for reasons you're in the slump. Again know, it's only because you are not giving 100% sales presentation. Don't let yourself get down; all that will do is to bring you further down.

Realize a slump is related to not doing as well as you did last month, or the months before, which should tell you, you can sell and the reason you are not now, is mainly because you are 'not' giving it 100% or more. Or maybe your sales pitch has become boring, or too long, or maybe it's because it's too serious? Or too many details, or maybe you have just become lazy.

Or you have forgotten how important it is to make sure you are always asking your customers the questions that will give you a 'yes' answer before you move on to the next point. Again, more on this later.

A Different Way Of Selling That Dares To Be Different

Always keep in mind, you alone caused this slump, and please never ever try to put the blame on anyone else. While in a slump the sale pitch needs to be looked at and new fresh energy, new ideas, and new ways to present your product or service must be found, and they will be found if you Dare To Become A Different Kind Of Salesperson and get rid of your outdated pitch.

Also, one of the hardest parts while in a slump is separating yourself from those who have been listening to you complain and help you justify why you have not been selling. For some reason this makes salespeople feel better about themselves. For some reason in society, it seems easier for bad influences to bring us down rather than for us to bring bad influences up.

So if you're serious about getting back to selling and begin making more sales and more money, then you need to either stay to yourself so you can keep yourself up and positive, or find, and then stay with people who you hope to become like.

You never see the top producers hanging out all day with the negative non- performers in your office, or anyplace you happen to work. You generally see the Dare To Be Different Salespeople with other winners, and negative people with the other negative people.

Also it is a good idea to take yourself off the sales floor for a few days, if you can, and really take a good look into what you are, or are not doing, from your meet and greet, all the way to the close. Most important you must fully understand you cannot keep doing what you have been doing, knowing it is clearly not working for you.

So, after looking into yourself, and into your sales pitch you should be able to find out what it is in you and in the pitch that has been left out, and if not left out, then what has not been given enough attention. Doing so will help you get out of the dreaded slump.

Also, in my opinion, I do believe that if someone is in a slump they should try to go away for a few days. Go away and completely forget your job. Just really enjoy your mini vacation. Or go out to a lovely dinner. Buy something for yourself. Most important, keep your mind off your job. Just fully enjoy yourself for a few days.

However, the best remedy to get out of a slump is for you to become a modern Dare To Be Different Kind Of Salesperson and design a Different Kind Of Selling Show Presentation.

A 'selling show presentation' is different from a pitch. Real different. A 'selling show' actually lets customers see everything that is being said, just like when watching any show (more on this later) along with a new positive, confident, energized you.

Also as this new Dare To Be Different Salesperson, you will able to understand customers in a whole new way. They

A Different Way Of Selling That Dares To Be Different

will no longer be just a way to a paycheck, they will become people who you really do want to help, and you will find you will want to treat each customer the same way you would want to be treated, if you were the customer.

So, is it time to change your outdated sales pitch and replace it with a Different Kind Of Selling Presentation? Absolutely yes. So if you do decide that yes, you do want to be a Dare To Be Different Kind Of Salesperson, then after you have made your needed changes to your new Different Kind Of Selling, and you feel you are ready to start delivering your new selling show, do so.

Put yourself back out on the sales floor and implement the new Dare To Be Different You and your new Different Kind Of Selling. A show worthy of an award and the award is the sale.

And Yes You Will Sell Again As A
DARE TO BE DIFFERENT SALESPERSON
Having A
DIFFERENT KIND OF SELLING PRESENTION

A Dare To Be Different Salesperson

You have something to sell. Whatever it is, your job as a very Dare To Be Different Kind Of Salesperson is to be able to 'show' your customers how your product or service will help them enjoy their jobs more. As this new very different salesperson you are in the business to 'serve' the people whom you are dealing with.

The Dare To Be Different Salesperson does not believe it is their job to get customers money. Their job is 'show' customers instead of selling them, and so their job is to do their best to 'show 'customers 'value' for their money.

Value in some way, for it is the key to the sale and in doing so you will get out of the habit of customer challenge if

A Different Way Of Selling That Dares To Be Different

they do not buy, and instead get in the habit of self challenge. Your customers really want you to care about them and their needs. And customers want to know the value of owning what is being sold.

Now it's time to find out what makes a Dare To Be Different Kind Of Salesperson. A Dare To Be Different Salesperson is constantly sharpening their selling presentations, making sure they are up to date with customers and their needs. All the time, because the greater the selling presentation, the easier the sell. The easier the sell, the more sales. The more sales, the more money they make.

A Dare To Be Different Salesperson will never will be like others and they know most, if not all sales people have a set fixed presentation. They have been trained on product knowledge, what to say and when to say it. So their sales pitches come across as canned.

That is why these very different salespeople will never have a canned pitch, they will have Different Kinds Of Selling Show Presentations. More on this later.

Another important thing, this very different kind of salesperson never prejudges a customer. If you are prejudging your customer because of how they look, their age, or whatever, it is that prejudgment that could well cost you the sale. You never really know if any customer has money or not.

I remember when I started my first job in sales, my first customer was a single lady. Up front she told me she was recently fired from her job, and had no money at this time. So instead of giving up right then, I went ahead and Dared To Be Different and did my entire Different Selling Show Presentation, and she ended up buying. She had called her brother and borrowed the money from him. So, never prejudge.

Like most normal salespeople a Dare To Be Different Salesperson knows their product inside and out, but unlike other salespeople they will only tell what a customer needs to hear, for why bore and waste time on things that are not reverent to a customer? They only show the features that have value for that customer, then sell the benefits of those features.

To repeat and this is so important, the Dare To Be Different Salesperson likes to know different meanings for certain words. They believe that by knowing those meanings they can better create Different Selling Show Presentations which include 'different' ways to counter the customer's objections before they arise, and that is another reason why they use a dictionary.

Do you or any salespeople you know use a dictionary in helping with the sales process? If not, you should, for the understanding what a word means, other than what one was told, is far more than a sales trainer can give you, for they give the outdated ways to sell. In most cases that is.

A Different Way Of Selling That Dares To Be Different

Again, we already know that by using a dictionary, the Dare To Be Different Kind Of Salesperson finds different word meanings, and they use those different word meanings to help them design new original ways to do their own Different Kind Of Selling Show Presentations.

For example, according to the dictionary, the word 'salesperson' comes from two words, 'sales and person.' So let's look at them. A meaning for the word 'sales' is, 'a special disposal of goods.'

That tells this Dare To Be Different Kind Of Salesperson that they need a 'special' way of selling their product or service. They need a 'special' Different Kind Of Selling Presentation. Presentations that do Dare To Be Different, from start to finish.

Another meaning for the word 'sales' is, an 'opportunity to sell.' A meaning for the word opportunity is 'a good time to obtain something.' And that is exactly what it does mean to the very different kind of salespeople. It is their opportunity to obtain the customers trust, sale, and then the customers returning business over the years.

They also believe the customer is an opportunity to proudly sell them something that will in some way improve their job, or some aspect of their life. So their job is to make sure customers know how their service or product will improve their job, or life in some way. Is what you sell able to improve some aspect of your customer's life? If not you may consider changing jobs.

Another example for the word 'sales' is, 'sale.' One meaning for the word, 'sale,' is to 'take.' Okay, that now tell this different kind of salesperson that they will need 'things' for their customer to take, which will make it easier for them to take the product or service at the end. Things? What does that mean? You will find out a little later. Read on.

Another meaning for the word, 'sale' is 'sell.' Looking at the word 'sell,' you find a meaning of, 'to promise.' This now tells the very different kind of salesperson that when they sell to someone, it's more than just selling, it's much more, it's making a promise to their customers.

Did you know that when you sell, you are making a promise? Understanding this, the very different kind of salesperson would never make promises they cannot deliver, and again, they never put the money first, instead they always put their customers first.

This very different kind of salesperson prides their self on making sure they do keep all promises they make. Doing so, makes them feel like they have done a good honest job of doing their highest sense of right and this causes them to take a deep breath, followed with a heartfelt real smile.

A Different Way Of Selling That Dares To Be Different

They take much pride in how completely 'different' they are in their approach to the selling game. Always. In fact they will let a customer walk before trying to sell a customer something they do not need, nor can really afford.

Yes, sometimes their boss does not like it if they let a customer walk, but then, as the boss thinks about it, this Dare To Be Different Kind Of Salesperson is always at the top of the sales line, then they smile and let it go.

A Dare To Be Different Kind Of Salesperson, unlike ordinary salespeople does not need to do much questioning into the customers current ways, for all they need to do is to find out what customer does and does not like about what they currently have and use. Even if it is a minor one, they find it. A few questions, yes, only a few will be needed, but questions that will not seem like you are probing.

Again, a very different kind of salesperson knows it is much easier to connect to a customer when you can insert a little laugher into your presentation. Don't you like it yourself when you have a fun salesperson working with you? This different kind of salesperson does loosen up while still being professional and they have fun making the sale.

Now let's look at another meaning for the second word in 'salesperson,' and we find one meaning which is the word, 'person.' Okay, so let's see a meaning for the word, 'person.'

One meaning for 'person,' is 'a human being who prefers something special.'

That means it is up to the very different kind of salesperson to make sure they do find something special about their product or service, and be sure to point it out to the customer. Remember, it must be something 'special,' even if it's something that may not be obvious.

If you were a very different kind of salesperson, you would only sell what you yourself would buy, if you ever needed that kind of product or service. And of course, had the money. Which you would have, if you become a Dare To Be Different Kind Of Salesperson.

To repeat, it should not be your job to put the money before the customer's real needs, so they never allow the money to be what it's all about, instead they make the customer and their needs are the first concern. Is that how you have thought about your selling? Or, have you thought the sale meant you would make money?

Again I stress, a very different kind of salesperson would never think of the money first. Never. They do want to first give their customer 'value' for their money along with making sure the product or service is right for them. This very different kind of selling is always, customers needs first.

A Different Way Of Selling That Dares To Be Different

As a very different kind of salesperson, they must always be on the lookout for boredom. To repeat, how often do you look for boredom in your customers? And again, it's easy to spot for it shows, just like enthusiasm shows. Yes, I know I repeat a lot, but that's okay. It does help things to register.

They also know today's customer is not the customer of the past. No, today's customers are choosier. They are harder to please. They want it fast, and they want more for less. Yes, they want the bottom line, now. So as a Dare To Be Different Salesperson, they make sure the bottom line is first.

What? No one puts the bottom line first? Yes, the Dare To be Different Salespeople do, well almost do give the bottom line up front. How? Why? Most things that are sold have different prices depending on what's included, so by giving customers the middle price you have hopefully taken that out of their mind for now, and now you will show them what you are selling, and they should want to listen, my customers always did.

Customers like it when they meet a Dare To Be Different Kind Of Salesperson, a look forward to seeing and hearing what else might surprise them. Think about that for a minute.

A very different kind of salesperson would like what they sell? And they would prefer their product over others? Why?

Because if you do not like your product, again, why are you selling it? Why are you promising your customer that what you sell is good, if you would not buy it, if you could?

And again, they will let the customer know and believe that they are the first priority and will then explain to their customer that they will be showing them 'value' for their money and then customer can decide if it is of value to or for them.

It is most important that the customer understands fully it will only be them that will be making the final decision, all based on their own needs and desire. No Dare To Be Different Salesperson would ever try to be the deciding factor in any sale. Never. Their main job is to show why it is best to have what they are selling, no, not selling, offering.

And another important factor is, they will always have a clean desk. A desk showing all the selling materials will instantly turn a customers off, so the very different kind of salespeople will have a small table or such slightly behind their desk where they keep the visual materials they will be showing as proofs of what they are, and have said.

One of the most important things for this different salesperson is to show, yes, 'show,' the customers what and how their product or service is different, and or superior to what customer currently have and use.

A Different Way Of Selling That Dares To Be Different

And should your product or service not be superior, then you must find at least one thing that is as good as customer's current product or service. This Different Kind Of Selling is known as, Visual Selling Show Presentations.

So, this word, 'show' is the 'key' to the entire Different Kind Of Selling Presentations. This very different kind of salesperson does understand how valuable any showing of visual proof is, and they will find that proof in some 'visible forms' and use them freely. And if you do not use a Visual Presentation Show, you should make one.

To repeat, this very different kind of salesperson understands how important it is to have things, anything, that can be handed to a customer. They will have some kind of visual facts to show the customers about the highlights of the product or service, or whatever it is they are offering the customer.

So yes, the Different Kind Of Selling is by using Visual Persuading. The entire selling show is designed with using visuals. Visual persuading is by far the best way to let the customer see what you are saying, as you say it. They love it, and once you start using them, you also will love using them. Customers like most people like a good show and will want to hear and watch it. Later on you will find out how to make one.

After customer accepts whatever is they are being offered, they have given their first 'ok.' The first 'yes,' if you will. This is very important. And very important that both take what is handed to them, if there are two or more people. And that is why it is important to use hands on visuals.

 ## Before Moving On

WE WILL BE LOOKING AT
'different'
WAYS TO HANDLE SOME THINGS AS A NEW
DARE TO BE DIFFERENT SALESPERSON

Reacting

Again, a Dare To Be Different Salesperson knows that it is their understanding of words and their different meanings that helps them sell more. So now we will see what we can find out about the words 'reacting.' That means it dictionary time again.

Starting with a few meanings for the word, 'react', we find the first meaning of, 'opponent.' Opponent? A Dare To Be Different Salesperson would never see their customers as an opponent. Do you see your customers as an opponent? If you do you will not be a top salesperson.

If you do see your customer as an opponent, then there will a winner and a loser. This is wrong. You both should be winners if the customer decides to purchase, or if they do not, it still matters to the very different salesperson that the customer is treated good with either decision they make.

A Different Way Of Selling That Dares To Be Different

Another meaning for the word 'react' is to be on the 'defensive.' What would any Dare To Be Different Salesperson have to be defensive about? Just because a customer gives an objection does not mean for you to react. How would you feel if you were the customer and a salesperson reacted to your objection?

When you react, which means to see the customer as an opponent, the customer will instantly feel this and will want to get away from you. So get to know yourself. Get to know how and why you react to what the customer does or does not do or say.

The next time you meet a customer and they hit your anger button or your impatience button and you start to react, stop the second you become aware that you are reacting as you always have.

The very different kind of salesperson knows it's only a habit, and remember, a habit can be changed. Now think, why do you react out of habit? You know you have a good product or service, so what could the customer possibly say to you to make you react and go on the defensive?

The customer's objection is just telling you have not convinced them your product or service is worth it. This is not the customers fault. It would be your job if you become a Dare To Be Different Salesperson to show the customer value and why they need your product or your service. Reacting will make any customer dislike you, and for you to dislike them. This serves on one.

A Dare To Be Different Salesperson does not get defensive when objections come their way. If you react in a negative or defensive way it then causes your customers to react the same way, then you are both on the defensive and nothing is going to happen. So the very different salesperson will always respond instead

So since the best thing for the different kind of salesperson to do, is to respond to the customer, and since they use a dictionary they understand what the word 'respond' means.

Responding

When you react to a customer, did it ever enter your mind to respond back to them with a question they could answer yes to? That is always the best way to respond. It is important to make a customer feel that what they have to say is valuable, even if it is an objection.

So in order to respond the very different kind of salesperson will know some meanings for the word. So yes, it is dictionary time again if you want to know how to respond instead of reacting.

The dictionary tells you the word 'respond' means an 'answer.' That tells you that when you respond to a customer, you must respond with a question to them, hopefully a question the customer can answer with a yes.

According to the dictionary another meaning for the word 'respond' is 'solution.' Solution has a meaning of, 'to solve.' Now this is a good meaning for the word 'solve', and that is to, 'remove.' Remove? Remove what?

A very different kind of salesperson understands that customers like it when you respond to them by removing doubts. No customer likes it when a salesperson reacts to them if they show doubts.

It is the job of a Dare To Be Different Salesperson to remove all customers doubts, and because they do use a Different Kind Of Selling Show Presentation, the doubts are fully addresses throughout the presentation show.

That is why it is so important that you respond positively to your customer instead of reacting to them as you answer their objections, and you do so by remembering what you said about their objection during the presentation and by restating it, and hopefully by doing this, you will be removing the doubts that cause the objection. Acting defensively will get you nowhere.

The dictionary also tells us another meaning for the word 'respond' is, 'to react favorably.' Knowing this, the Dare To Be Different Salesperson will always respond favorably each time a customer begins to bug them, and all through the selling show no matter what customer does, they respond favorably. Period.

A Different Way Of Selling That Dares To Be Different

Doing so, customer will realize you are not reacting unfavorably, and they begin liking you some, and that should stop them from wanting to bug you. This is by far the best way to deal with negative customers. In my opinion.

Ways in which you can respond. Soft smile and count silently to five before you speak. Its really important to say or do things to let customers know you like them. Offer them a visual that applies to their objection

These are but a few ways to respond, so you may want to Dare To Be Different and find some of your own new cool, unique different ways for you to respond favorably, no matter what customer does or said.

Knowing a little more about 'reacting' and 'responding' helps the Dare To Be Different Salesperson as they deal with the 'no's'. The 'no's are usually what causes someone to react instead of responding. That means it is a must to understand what a 'no' is really telling you, and that is another reason why a very different kind of salesperson will use a dictionary.

With that said, let's investigate the word

Handling The NO

A Dare To B Different Kind Of Salesperson is always excited by the challenge to go from the 'No, I'm not interested', to customer showing a lot of interest? This modern very different salesperson will never be fooled buy a 'no,' for they do understand, all the no's do is to force them to design a Different Kind Of Selling Show Presentation, one that will avoid the 'no's.'

NO is such a neat little word. It has the ability to tell you all about what your client is thinking and feeling. Each 'no' is telling you what you need to do, and how to do it. They are a great selling tool, if you understand what a 'no' is, and what it means, other than the one you have been taught, for there are different meanings.

To repeat, as people, we become accustomed to thinking of words in only one set of meaning. And again, words often have many meanings and by delving into the many different

A Different Way Of Selling That Dares To Be Different

meanings of words you will gain a new exciting way of viewing the world and especially the world of selling.

A very different kind of salesperson knows some of these different meanings. So, as with other chapters, we will begin the journey into the word 'no' by, yes, using the dictionary. Doing so, you will see how the small two-letter word called 'no' will take on many new meanings.

So instead of just hearing the word 'no,' the Dare To Be Different Salespeople have learned to know why the customer may be saying 'no', thereby being in a position to overcome it before it arises. Now let's look at some of the meanings for 'no' and as you will see, it becomes a very detoured road.

Dictionary Meanings For No

No Means
Disbelief

Knowing this 'no' means disbelief, then it is important to find out what it is a customer is disbelieving on their part. Now is a good time to ask a question that will get you a yes. You can say something like, 'Does this make sense to you.'

The answer you get will let you know it's okay to move on or to stay on the point you just stated. This is a good example of why the question for a 'yes' answer is always asked before moving on. No sense moving on if there is any disbelief in customers mind, on or about the point you just made.

No Means
To Decline

If all through the selling show presentation the customer is being offered things that they will take from you, and once

A Different Way Of Selling That Dares To Be Different

taken you must right then after the acceptance, have a question for your customer that they will have to answer 'yes' to. If you have two customers, be sure you get a yes from both of them. Do your best not to offer things they may decline.

This I think is very important because each time they 'take' from you, it is like a 'yes,' and then you get a second 'yes 'from a question that can only be answered by them with a 'yes,' and that means you just got two 'yes's.' So by the end of you presentation, it will be easier for them to again say 'yes.' Think about that for a minute.

No Means
Will Not Improve Life

For this 'no' you need be sure to point out how the product or service can and will improve customers life. Improve their job, improve something, because the customer does need to know why or how the product will improve something for them, and if not, why purchase?

Again, ask a question that customer will tell you how your product or service will improve how they are now doing things at home or work.

No Means
Doubt

At this 'no' the customer is rejecting the truths of what you have been telling them. This 'no' is letting you know the customer is not yet convinced what you are offering, is actually what you are saying it is.

Before the Different Kind Of Selling Show continues, you need to know where the doubts are, and then you need to eliminate them. The best way to do this is to ask a question about what they like best about your product or service. If they give you one, then you can continue to the next point you want to make.

Also, it could be they do not want to let you know they believe what you are saying because they might buy your product. So you would not want to accept this 'no' and end your 'selling show.'

No Means
Too Many Details

A 'no' happens when customer is overloaded with too many details. A Dare To Be Different Salesperson would never give a customer too many details, ever. So be sure not to give too many details, as it will confuse them and make them want to think.

No Means
Uncertain Of The Outcome

This 'no' is telling you your customer is' uncertain' about the outcome of owning your product, or service. So stop and

A Different Way Of Selling That Dares To Be Different

think, did you 'show' them what they could expect the outcome to be, if they purchased?

They must know for certain that the outcome will be better for them. This 'no' then will not arise if you do make customer certain of the outcome of owning.

Did you get them to agree that the outcome would be better for them to have your product or service, than not owning the product, before you moved on?

No Means
Does Not Know Enough

Hopefully this is not true, but if it is, you would have to find out what you missed. The customer must feel they do know enough. You must 'visually show' or give customer some brand new information from which they can use it to change their own mind.

No Means
Not A Fair Price

This 'no' can mean the customer does not feel you have a fair price. You will need to find out what he thinks is a fair price. So if you do not want a 'no' later, make sure that customer agrees that your product or service is a fair price. But first you will need to find out what he thinks is a fair price.

Now show the customer some comparisons. Have 'visual' information on other products or services, along with their prices. Have a question that must be answered with a yes, about the price.

No Means
No Benefits

Find a question that customer will agree, that yes, they can see the benefits. Have them tell you how they can see that your product or service will benefit them in some way. This is very important that they do see the benefits before you reach the end of the selling show.

No Means
Inconsistent

No's can come when you are not consistent with what you have been saying. That is why it is most important to use 'visuals' to prove what you are saying. Also, you may want to check all 'four' of your Different Kinds Of Selling Show Presentations for any inconsistencies.

No Means
No Interest

This 'no' tells you that your customer neither sees nor hears anything of interest for them. So this 'no' is saying there was

A Different Way Of Selling That Dares To Be Different

something missing in the 'selling show presentation' and it did not get, nor keep customers interest. Not customers fault.

There must have been some interest, or why are they with you? A very different kind of salesperson knows that because the customer is there with them, then there was some interest of some kind when they came in. So it must be you not knowing what to show them.

No Means
Not Important To Them

For this 'no' you need to make sure the customer does see and understands how and why your product is important for them. There must be 'one thing' about your product or service that you can get them to admit, yes, it is important to them.

Create a question that they will answer 'yes' to. Remember, never move on until you have at least one 'yes.' From both, if there are two.

No Means
No Value To Them

This 'no' is now letting you know that your customer does not think what you are trying to sell them has any value to them. This is not the fault of the customer.

Dare To Be Different Salespersons main goal is to show customers the value of owning the product or the service being offered. Figure out some question to ask them that should give you a 'yes.' Try to stay until you get a few 'yes's' about the value.

No Means
Insignificant-Not Important

This 'no' is now letting you know that your customer does not think what you are trying to sell him has any importance to them. So if important means, 'personal status,' this 'no' means that your customer does not feel your product will do anything for his personal status. At home or at work.

Your customer believes you have nothing that will make them look better to their friends, other employees, or their boss. So now your approach must be to let them understand and see how the product or service will indeed, give them some kind of personal status.

No Means
Refusal

A dictionary meaning for refusal is, 'not allowing.' Do you not allow your customer to talk? Are you not allowing your customers to participate with you? You need your customer to be allowed to participate in the 'selling show presentation,' as it will then be, 'them,' helping in selling them.

A Different Way Of Selling That Dares To Be Different

A dictionary meaning for allow is, 'to admit.' Then this 'no' means they do not want to admit that what you have is something they might want. A good meaning for 'admit' is 'to accept.' There are many ways to overcome this 'no.'

One silly way is to ask them if it were free, would they take it. So your job would be to make customer want what you have, and then for customer to admit, that yes, they would take it for free.

Once the customer admits they would take the product for free, they are about ready to accept it as their own, and you have done your job. You should be pulling out your contracts and offering you hand.

No Means
Denial

Dictionary has a meaning for 'denial,' and it is, 'to reject.' At this 'no' the customer is rejecting the truths of what you have been telling them.

Or their 'no' could be the customer letting you know they do not want to let you know they believe what you are saying because they might buy your product.

So you would not want to accept this 'no' and end your selling show. Instead, ask any question that will get you that 'yes' answer, then move on.

No Means
Disagreement

One dictionary meaning for 'disagreement' is, 'inconsistent.' So again the 'no' is letting you know you have not been consistent in your 'selling show presentation' and the customer feels your details are not matching up with the words you have been speaking.

They can see or hear inconsistencies. This frightens customer and off sets their desire for your product. You have probably lost your sale with this 'no.'

No Means
No Trust

At this 'no' you need to know what it is that they do not trust. Find out what it is they do not trust? You? Your company? Your product? You? Then ask some kind of question, that hopefully will get you a 'yes,' answer.

Never move on until you have at least one 'yes' about the trust and about the information you have just given them. If no 'yes' can be had, the suggestion here would be to thank the customer for their time, and leave as fast as you can. No trust, no sale.

That's enough about the NO.

So now you know a little more about why customers say the word 'no.' Knowing these different meanings you should

A Different Way Of Selling That Dares To Be Different

never again be fooled by the 'no's'. All the 'no's' do is to force you to make a better, and most important, a Very Different Kind Of Selling Presentation that does avoid those 'no's.'

Remember, you can never blame the customer if they say 'no,' because customer said 'no' because you did not show them enough value or benefit's. Not enough reasons to say, yes. Again, not customers fault.

A 'no' cannot be changed, at least not until the person saying no has a reason to change their mind. Without this reason, you can be sure they will not change their mind. Therefore you must supply them just that reason.

All those 'no's' can be used to ask questions. The questions in most cases will be just another way to have the customer help you sell your product or service to them. If the questions require the 'yes' answer.

A Dare To Be Different Salesperson uses the different meanings for the 'no', and covers all of them in every selling show. They understands they will have those 'no's', and also understands that they help guide them to overcoming reason for customer not to buy. Understanding 'no's' will help with selling the 'four personalities.'

Personalities

It is the job of any very different kind of salesperson to understand some of the different personalities that they will be encountering. The reason for knowing different personalities is for the purpose of helping to know which 'selling show' is best for their current customer and their personality.

The Dare To Be Different Salesperson knows that if they have only one 'selling show presentation' they are missing a lot of sales. Why? To repeat, it is because there are many different types of customers. Therefore it is very important that there should be more than 'one selling show presentation.'

A Dare To Be Different Kind Of Salesperson will individualize their Very Different Kind Of Selling Show Presentations to match the customers personality, knowing there are many different types of customers with many types of personalities, therefore it is necessary to have more than one 'selling show.'

A Different Way Of Selling That Dares To Be Different

It is up to the very different kind of salesperson to put together a very 'different' way to present their selling show that works with the different personalities, because the customers will be different.

That means, this unique 'very different kind of salesperson' will create at least 'four different' ways to present their selling show. One for each of the four main types of personalities.

# The Four Personalities

Type 'A' Personality

You must be totally organized to make them feel comfortable. The type 'A' personality loves to be in control. This customer is also impatient, so you must be quick giving your selling show. That means it is necessary to keep your show moving fast and smooth, so there isn't much chance in customer taking over.

You do not worry about the details with this customer, as they just do not care about them. With this personality, get to the bottom line as fast as possible as they bore easily. But they always ask this impatient customer a question that will get them a 'yes' reply before they move on.

The type 'A' customer loves change, so this Dare To Be Different Salesperson will be sure to let customer know the changes their product or service will provide to and for their

A Different Way Of Selling That Dares To Be Different

customer. Also this personality needs to see how they will save time by having the product or service.

The very different kind of salesperson should not have a problem with this personality if they are using their different out of the box customer designed Different Selling Show Presentations, with visuals. Visuals that they have designed just for this personality.

Again, it is very important to get to the bottom line as fast as possible, for this customer does bore easily, but the visuals still must be used. More on visuals later.

Do You Have A Different Kind Of Selling Show For This Customer?

Type 'B' Personality

This customer wants to be liked. That means that throughout the 'selling show,' they must know, that yes, they are liked. The best way to do this is to do this is through words or actions that can show this customer, they are liked.

The 'B' personality customer needs and wants to be excited. This customer also likes enthusiasm, so it is important to show lots of excitement along with lots of enthusiasm, and to keep it all throughout the 'selling show presentation.'

Do not bother with details with a type 'B' personality. That means that throughout the 'selling show presentation', no giving any details about the product or service. Leave out the details. This customer does not care about them. Details will cause them to lose interest, quickly.

The type 'B' personality customer loves new concepts. So you must find something new about product or service, and instantly let customer know that your product or service is, or has something new or different about it. Then use a 'visual' to prove it.

The type 'B' personality loves and accepts change, and they thrive on things creative, so this customer will really love

A Different Way Of Selling That Dares To Be Different

your Very Different Kind Of Selling Show Presentation, and this show will make this customer so much more receptive to saying 'yes,' when that last 'yes' is needed.

Also it is important to make sure this customer can 'see' some new concept about the product or the service being offered. Again, it is important to use 'visuals' to show them. And always ask this customer after each stated point, some question that will get them to say 'yes.'

**Do You Have A
Different Kind Of Selling Show
For This Customer?**

The Type 'C' Personality

Unlike the customers who do not need details, this customer needs all the details. They need all the information. So it is best to give some details at the end of each short paragraph, then be sure to ask a question that will get a 'yes' answer, then move on to the next detail.

The type 'C' personality, like the 'A' personality, will do their best to take control. The good news is, if you are using a unique Very Different Kind Of Selling Presentation there is almost no opportunity for this to happen.

This customer must be 'shown' how this will fit better than what they are currently doing or using. This is important because they do not want to change how they are, and have been doing things. They like routine.

Understanding this, a Dare To Be Salesperson will 'show' and explain that customer does not have to change, but instead, will have a better experience with your product or service. So 'show' them. Yes, 'show.' How? By using 'visuals.' Again, more on visuals later.

This type 'C' personality customer will want to 'see' what other buyers have to say about the product or service being

A Different Way Of Selling That Dares To Be Different

offered. The rightly created 'visuals' can show them. Also stress how wonderful your customer service is. That's very important to them.

**Do You Have A
Very Different Kind Of Selling Show
For This Customer?**

Type D Personalities

To make the type 'D' customer feel comfortable, your office and desk must be clean, as they do not like clutter. If there is stuff all over the desk, the interest of this customer is instantly lost.

This customer does not want to be friends, so do not try to get to know this customer. Do not talk about their personal life, at all. Instead the 'selling show' will start off with facts. Facts will be the focus of this customers 'selling show presentation'.

That is why this Different Kind Of Selling has been designed entirely based on 'facts', because it will be the facts that this customer is given, and they will be used to help them make a decision about your product or your service.

It is important that after each short paragraph to go back over the 'facts,' making sure this customer has no questions left about what they just heard and seen. Then, they are asked a question that they must answer 'yes' to.

The type 'D' personality will look for the worst serrano, if they should buy product or service. This customer also does not like change and will resist it, so it is important to make

A Different Way Of Selling That Dares To Be Different

sure they have seen how it will not change what they are used to. But instead, will only make it better.

Only after this customer has a sufficient amount of 'facts' will they feel comfortable making a 'yes' decision, so it is important to not rush them into making a choice, but instead learn to be comfortable with a little social awkwardness on their part.

To repeat, this customer cannot be rushed, so take it slow, and like with all the other three personalities, be sure the visuals are used, and that before you move on to the next fact, you ask the question that will give you a 'yes'. That is, if you are now, one of the Dare To Be Different Kind Of Salesperson.

**Do You Have A
Very Different Kind Of Selling Show
For This Customer?**

Knowing Customer Concerns

It is very important that as this very different kind of salesperson that you take each of these customers concerns and work them into your 'selling show presentation.' If you do not, you will most likely will end up with the 'no' you do not want to hear at the end.

It is also very important; I believe to have a few different ways to 'show 'your customer, just in case the first one doesn't get you, your 'yes.' It might be good to know a meaning or two for these words.

Why is good to know word meaning? Again, because knowing some different meanings for each word, you will have a better understanding and that understanding will help you to be able to present it to your customer in ways they have not heard before. So, it's dictionary time again.

Customer Concerns Samples

What VALUE Is There For Me

From Dictionary

Value:
Importance

That now shows you that you can use the word importance to show the customer value. You could say something about the importance of why they should have your product or service. Using the word 'important' should help customer listen a bit closer, if something is important to them.

Find something that you can show 'value,' it does not matter how little there is, it must be presented in some way. Why would anyone want to purchase something if there was no value. Show them some 'value/ and then ask, 'John, can you see the value of owning this?

Another meaning for 'value' is 'worth.' This should be an easy one to use in your Different Kind Of Selling, for to be able to say to customer, wouldn't it be worth it to be able to, (their need) You would use this for the product or service you are selling, offering.

Remember, you must always ask a question about the word you are using, and make sure you ask a question the customer should answer yes to, before moving on.

How Can It IMPROVE My Life

According to the dictionary a meaning for the word 'improve' is, 'to make good use of. This is a good meaning, and is easy to add into your Different Kind Of Selling Presentations. You can first 'show' your customer ways your product or service can improve their life, their job, home, car, or whatever it is your are offering to them.

And this meaning of 'improve' will be easy when it's time to ask the 'yes' question, You could say, 'John, can you see how owing this can improve your life? If you get a 'yes' quickly move on, however, if there is a hesitation, ask the question in a different way, like you could say, Or, Tom, can you see how you could and would make good use of this? Once you hear the 'yes,' move on.

A Different Way Of Selling That Dares To Be Different

How USEFUL Will It Be For Me

One dictionary meaning for useful is, 'serving some purpose.' This also is a good meaning and you should be able to 'show' your customer some purpose that your product or service will or can do. Show them some little thing that will be useful and then ask, 'John, can you see how useful this product or service will be, to and for you? Remember; stay until you get some kind of a 'yes' answer.

What Are The BENEFITS For Me

From the dictionary you find a meaning for 'benefit' of 'advantage.' You will first show customer the benefits and then ask, 'John can you see the advantage you'll get by owning this product?' Again, if it's a fast yes, move on, but if there is any hesitating, re ask your question in different words. First point out some 'advantage' to the customer if they had you product or service, one you know will get you the 'yes,' then move on.

How Can I PROFIT From Owing

The word 'profit' has the same meaning as, the one for 'benefits,' and that is, 'advantage.' So this concern is the same as the benefit one, so you would respond in the same manner. And you can in some way 'show' the customer how they can profit if they buy your product or service? Show anything 'visual' that they can see as proof, and then ask, 'John can you see how it will profit you to own?

If the hesitant 'yes' is there, re ask the question by first explaining why and how the customer can profit by having this product or service and then explain the 'advantages,' then ask customer to tell you one advantage. Then move on.

How Do I Know I Can Trust You.

It is completely up to you as a Dare To Be Different Kind Of Salesperson to establish trust in your clients. Only you can do this, then you must assure your customer that they can trust the name of your company. Use 'visuals' for your proof. Be sure you do not move on until you hear the 'yes' to your question based on trust.

Again, any hesitating, ask a different question about you being there after the purchase to help them, do not move on until they agree that 'yes' they do believe you will be there to help them. Only then do you move on.

What Real ASSURANCE Do I Have
Assurance
Dictionary tells us assurance means a 'promise'

You must always assure customer that your product or service is good for them in some way and then ask, 'John do you see how owing this will help you accomplish (whatever it is he is buying it for)

A Different Way Of Selling That Dares To Be Different

One meaning for the word 'assurance' is, 'promise.' If customer hesitates for a second, quickly restate one or two of the promises you have made earlier. Then restate why your product or service is for them and or their company. Restate it so your changes of a 'yes' are pretty good. Then move on.

What If It Doesn't Work As You Say
Dictionary says work means 'accomplish'

Your customer will be thinking this, so it has to be addressed, and in a very different kind of way. Again, after 'showing' customer how your product or service will work for them, you must ask them if they see how it will. Once more, ask the 'yes' question, like, 'do you see how it will work as I have said.'

Meaning for the word, 'work' is 'accomplish.' So if the yes is slow, quickly ask the question in a different way. First you will explain how it will accomplish what it is suppose to accomplish, then ask something like, 'Do you see how my product or service can accomplish what you need? Now, cross your fingers and hope you hear the 'yes.'

How Can It ACCOMPLISH What I Want

This is so important for your customer to know. Do your best to explain how it will accomplish their need and then, somehow you must have your customer explain to you how they will use your product or service to 'accomplish' their need.

Then you could hopefully come up with something funny to say, then ask, If I gave this to you, would you take it. Now you get your 'yes' and move on.

How Is Product Or Service Superior To Others?

You must find something, anything about your product or service that is 'superior' to others, followed by, 'John, can you see how this product is superior to others? Again, if you do not get an instant 'yes,' do not move on.

Instead, repeat something about your product or service that is somehow different and then show it to your customer in a 'visual form', then ask something like, 'That's good, isn't it? Hopefully you will hear the 'yes.'

The above are only a few samples of customers concerns and need to be built into your 'selling show.' Sprinkle them throughout and by doing so, you will not have your customer expressing or thinking of them. YOU, handle them before they come up. Never wait for customer to express or think of negative things, handle them before they come up.

These Are A Few Samples Of Some Of
The POINTS That Need to Covered In Every
Very Different Kind Of Selling Presentation
If You Do Not, You Will Have The NO'S

How To Design Selling Show Presentations

The secret to Different Kind Of Selling Show Presentations is, they must be a Visual Selling Show Presentations. Yep. A Visual Selling Show. From start to finish, it's all visual. In reality it is VISUAL PERSUADEING.

There are many things you must do if you really want to be a new Dare To Be Different Kind Of Salesperson, and what is that? To better understand some word meanings, for they do help getting the yes's you need throughout the 'selling show presentation'.

For example, if you are, or are going to be doing Different Kind Of Selling Show Presentations, you will need to understand what the word 'presentation' means.

Using the dictionary again, you will find the word 'presentation' means, 'now in view.' Therefore the 'selling show presentation' of your product or service must be made so when it comes into view of your customer, it has been designed to make your customer want to view it, which means to watch it. To listen to it.

The dictionary also tells you the word 'presentation' means, 'under consideration.' The new and Very Different Kind Of Selling Presentation Shows of your product or service is designed to bring into 'view' what you want the customer to consider, as they view your selling show. The selling show is to let your customer view your product in a brand new way.

Once again, the Very Different Kind Of Selling Show Presentations are also called, Visual Persuading. Visual persuading will help the sale along, so create a new way to present your own 'visual show.' Remember, your 'show 'is for the purpose of 'showing' and proving all that you are saying.

The Different Kind Of Selling is and must be alive and exciting, and that comes from lots of enthusiasm and from lots of excitement. The 'show' must be 'original,' so remember that as you begin to designing your own 'selling show.'

It is important to understand the Selling Show must be something the customers have never seen. Each and every Different Selling Show Presentation must be personally

A Different Way Of Selling That Dares To Be Different

designed for each of the 'four personalities.' No one selling show covers all customers, and that is the reason for more than one presentation show.

The Dare To Be Different Kind Of Salesperson makes sure their entire Different Selling Show Presentation is designed for the customers to 'see' how good it is for them to own what is being offered. Not selling. Offering. You see people are more open to something being offered, even at a cost, rather than being sold something. No winner. No loser. Just an exchange.

The Different Kind Of Selling is to let the customer view your product in a brand new way. No matter what it is being sold, so this new Dare To Be Different Kind Of Salesperson finds new and different ways to present it, knowing the 'selling show', again is for the purpose of 'showing and proving,' all that is being said. Never too much repeating, it just helps it go deeper into the mind.

A Very Different Kind Of Selling Show Presentation Show must be something that will entertain as the show moves along. They believe their Different Kind Of Selling Show should be a bit bold, edgy, even a bit shocking, and the reason is to ensure customer attention. And, it certainly must be fun for both you and your customers. Who wants to sit and watch and listen to a boring show?

Make a list of all the reasons a buyer would want to buy your product or service. Think of every single one. Write them down. Memorize them. Once done, incorporate them into the selling show, both verbally and then visually.

Make another list of reasons why a customer would want to wait. To think it over. Try to think of all the reasons, and then again, work all of them into the 'selling show presentation,' and make sure you find some 'visuals' to use also. Yes, more on visuals later.

Next make another list of any fears a customer may have. Again, think of every fear someone could have about owning your product or service. Obvious ones along with little ones.

Then, yes, go back and add them into the new Different Selling Show Presentation. Then ask yourself, what are your promises? Write them down. Memorize then and then add them to your new Different Kind Of Selling Show Presentations.

Your 'selling show presentations' must handle the negatives of your product before the customer can bring them up. That means to make another list of every know negative a customer could think of. Figure out a way to make them seem not so important and incorporate them into your custom Different Selling Show Presentations.

Now one more time, make a list of all the 'benefits' of owning the product or the service? Write them down. Memorize them. Add each one to your new 'selling show presentation.'

A Different Way Of Selling That Dares To Be Different

The benefits are one of the most important things for a customer to hear, and most important, to see and hear all through the 'selling show.'

Again, it is most important that the entire above are sprinkled all through the Different Selling Show Presentation. Do not sit and give each one all at once. They must be voiced all through the show. It seems to help them sink it in. Just like all my repeating.

If a customer hears you bringing up little negative concerns here and there, negatives they could be thinking about, and not try to handle them at the end. Hearing them during presentation and by you, helps the customer to not be so concerned at the back end. This is true will all the above also. Again, just insert each of the good and bad all through the 'selling show presentation' instead of each one, all at once at the end.

After you have designed the new Different Kind Of Selling Show Presentation, then find someone to practice all 'four' of your 'selling show presentations' with. And again, yes, yes there are more than one 'selling show presentation.' Remember there are at least four.

The Different Kind Of Selling Show Presentations should be taped, and each one of the 'four' should be watched and carefully listened to. Doing this, you can see how you look, act and sound to customers. You can also see if it is in any way boring.

After taping yourself, look and listen for anything boring and really not needed, or if you talked to long on one thing, and watch to see how different you were while giving it.

If you find a single thing missing from the 'show,' be sure to go back and redo it, adding the missing parts, or just tweaking it some, if needed.

Being a Dare To Be Different Kind Of Salesperson will be fun for you and certainly fun for the customers, customers who are so bored and tired of the same old sales pitches. This unique Very Different Kind Of Selling makes selling so much easier and so much more fun for both you and your customers.

Once you start giving your Different Kind Of Selling Show Presentations to customers, it might be a good idea to really look at your 'sales presentation in person. How? You may want to video yourself doing your new presentations with live clients. Oh, you do have to ask your customer if it's okay if you film the presentation. Some will say yes and some will say no.

I did just that, I filmed myself giving my Dare To Be Different Sales Presentations from start to finish, and boy was I surprised. I was doing and saying things that could of, and should have been done or said elsewhere in my presentation, and some not done or said at all with this particular customer.

I found that actually being able to see and hear my presentation was the best thing ever, and as I became aware of what

A Different Way Of Selling That Dares To Be Different

I was actually doing wrong, I made sure I corrected whatever they were, and then I would re film myself, and I did this many times, until I felt there was nothing else I should change.

By doing all the above, and I did, it changed the rest of my selling career, and doing the video presentation with a few different customers, is how I ended up being a, Dare To Be Different Salesperson, doing a Very Different Kind Of Selling Show Presentations for the next 25 years, and making me one of the TOP SALESPEOPLE in my industry.

It is so important to have a Different Kind Of Selling Show Presentation, so all the above is important to understand, because, yes, customers today have heard ever type of sales pitch you can imagine, and that is why they will never be bored with you or your Different Kind Of Selling Show.

To end, I can't stress the importance that all through the entire Different Kind Of Selling Show there must be some kind of a 'visual' for each point being presented. All you say, needs a backup 'visual.'

**Now Last But Most Important For A
Dare To Be Different Salesperson
Is
Did My Customer Have A Good Experience
With Or Without Buying.**

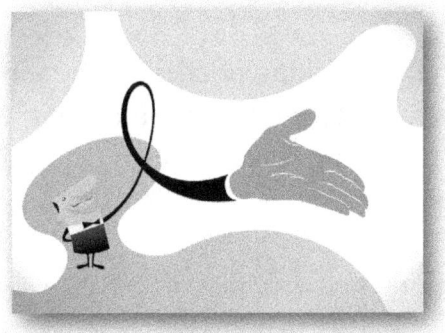

Act 1
The Different Approach

Dare To Be Different Salespeople are self starters. They create their own Different Kind Of Selling Show Presentations and they totally understand it is the 'opening of the show' that will help determine the sale.

If your 'selling show presentation' starts out the same way every other salesperson starts off, your customer will automatically shut off their mind.

This new approach to the old outdated sales pitches is known as a Different Kind Of Selling. This new approach begins with the Dare To Be Different Salesperson who is the star of the show and is 'different' in all ways from the outdated salespeople's pitches.

This very different kind of salesperson must be 'different' from the moment they meet a customer, for they fully understand, it is the first impression of them that sets the mood for the entire show.

Remember, there is only one first chance to make the first impression and that first impression should have something about it to generate some real interest from the customer,

A very different kind of salesperson gets totally 'excited' with each new customer, for it is their chance to Dare To Be Different as a salesperson. So unlike the ordinary salesperson, the Dare To Be Different Kind Of Salesperson wants to stand out from other sales people. In all ways. They never want to look or sound like all any other salespersons.

They know how important it is that their Different Kind Of Selling Show must have some little things that are 'shocking', shocking in a good way, right from the beginning of the meet and greet.

An example could be things or sayings that will make the customer want to be with you, and want to listen closely, wondering, what's next, and by you Daring To Be Different, will ensure customers full attention throughout the entire 'selling show.'

Once again, it will be fun for you and certainly fun for your customers, those customers who are so bored and tired of

A Different Way Of Selling That Dares To Be Different

the same old selling pitches This new modern customer will 'want' to watch your Different Kind Of Selling Show, if for nothing else, but to see what's next.

Oh, be sure your 'selling show' has parts that will cause a customer to 'laugh.' Why? Because customers are people, and most people, like to laugh. Plus it is so much easier to connect to your customer when you can insert laughter into your 'selling show,' plus a little laughter will help relax a customer.

This Dare To Be Different Salesperson knows that they must design their 'selling shows' to be 'exciting,' and so 'different' from any other kind of sales presentation, and doing so, you will find the more customers will admire you. They will like that you think in a new, Dare To Be Different, Out Of The Box way, and that you took the time to do so.

If you were a customer, wouldn't it be nice and fun to be greeted by a Dare To Be Different Kind Of Salesperson, doing a fast and Very Different Kind Of Sales Presentation? If it were you, wouldn't you want to find out what else they might surprise you with, after the 'different' way they met and greeted you? I would.

And how will this Dare To Be Different Kind Of Salesperson do all this? By giving the customer their special Different Kind Of Selling Shows. Selling Shows that totally shock, amaze, impress and entertains customers.

Dare To Be Different Kind Of Selling Shows, are one's a customer has never seen. And by the way, it is really kind of fun to design and create your own unique Dare To Be Different Selling Shows. And most fun is in giving them.

It is also very important for the Dare To be Different Salesperson to be very 'different' in all things pertaining not only to the 'selling show,' but also to them. Think, how different you are in how you first meet your customers. Again, are you creative and different, or are you like most others?

Next, our Dare To Be Different Kind Of Salesperson is very good at getting the 'full attention' of their customers from the first meet and greet. This Dare To Be Different Salesperson will never, ever start their 'selling show' if they do not have the full attention of both people, if more than one.

They know that if they do not have customers full attention they will most likely get the 'no,' at the back end. Full attention during the entire show is a must, and these Dare To Be Different Salespersons are also very good at keeping it. For keep it you must, if you want to get a 'yes' at the end.

A Dare To Be Different Kind Of Salesperson not only must look neat and clean, and again, I believe, a bit 'edgy', or at least 'different' in some way because they know their

A Different Way Of Selling That Dares To Be Different

appearance is the first thing a customer notices, and they do not want to look like a salesperson, and so by being 'different' they can instantly set themselves apart from the rest.

So again, think, are you creative in your personal appearance? As a Dare To Be Different Salesperson you make it a point to have something about you that will draw the customer's attention to 'IT' as you approach a customer.

Understanding this, you will need something 'bold', something completely 'different'. Something possibly customers have never seen before. Something that will instantly get their attention and cause them to sit up and take notice of you and what you have to say.

If you do not have something 'unique' or just 'different,' then you should go find something or have something made. It does not need to be expensive, just 'different.'

Your look could be a one of a kind, pin, ring, tie, dress, blouse, or anything that is totally different and would cause the customer to notice it, and instantly gets customers attention. Your attire should alsostand out.

When the Very Different Kind Of Salesperson and hopefully it's you, captures customer's attention in a totally 'different' way, and yes you will still have to look professional, but only in a Dare To Be Different Way, the customer will admire your unique approach and look, and that will help in having them want to watch and to listen to what you have to say.

Another important thing this very different kind of salesperson does understand, is what their customer may be thinking. Things like, 'How long is this going to take.' Along with, 'What kind of pressure will I be getting?' Or 'will you make me feel bad if I don't buy today.'

This Dare To Be Different Salesperson will tell the customer that there will not, under any circumstances be any pressure at all. Period. This statement said with excitement should help a customer break down their walls of resistance.

Doing this, customers will subconsciously begin to feel comfortable with you and then they will also be able to focus more on what you have to say. They will also wonder, what's next, since they have been told, it will be a DIFFERENT KIND OF SELLING EXPEREINCE.

By starting out this way, you will instantly get even more interest from the customer, and again, their curiosity will want them to want to see and hear what you have to say, that's 'different'. Wouldn't it be nice to have a customers 'want' to stay and listen and watch your 'selling show'?

A Different Way Of Selling That Dares To Be Different

Knowing this is how a customer is thinking and feeling, this Dare To Be Different Kind Of Salesperson will right up front let his customers know that this is not a 'sales pitch presentation', no, it is a Different Kind Of Selling and they are told, 'it should be fun and really different,'

Then smile and nod your head up and down. Most likely you will get a smile back from your customers. Smiles make a customer like you. Doing this customers subconsciously begin to feel comfortable with you and then they will also focus more on what you have to say as they know it is all for their best interest.

It is also very important that all throughout the Different Kind Of Selling Show Presentation you make sure the customer is really listening, and they will if you Dare To Be Different in you 'selling show.'

And it is most important that the one doing the 'selling show,' meaning you, also listens to the customers, and then somewhere during the 'selling show,' you will repeat some of the things the customer asked or said earlier. Doing this will impress the customer, which will cause the customer to like this very different kind of salesperson.

And once again I have to repeat, as this is the most important part of the Very Different Kind Of Selling Presentation Shows, the shows must be,

EXCITING. EDGY. BOLD. FUN. DIFFERENT.
Doing so will help have the customers full attention, but only if the
ENTIRE SHOW IS ENTERTAINING.
This Very Different Kind Of Selling follows through the entire show being,
FAST, FRESH, AND OH SO DIFFERENT.

Example Of The Different Approach

Say I'm going shopping, and I enter a clothing store, furniture store, car showroom, or whatever, and as I enter, I see a salesperson heading towards me and I think, oh no and turn in a different direction.

Then I hear, 'Hi, may I help you? How many times have I heard, 'Hi, may I help you?' I instantly think, oh no, here we go again. It bugs me and sometimes irritates me. I say no, I'm just looking and move away quickly. Most times the salesperson will follow me, then I have to make it plain to them, if I need you, I will come find you.

Well that's how your customers feel and think if you greet them with the same old line. 'Hi, I'm Tom, can I help you,' or Hi, I'm Tom and I'll be showing your around today. For me that is an instant turnoff. What is new and 'different' about that greeting? But how would I feel if it was a really Dare To Be Different greeting? Well it would certainly get my attention and my interest.

It's different when someone meets a Dare To Be Different Salesperson. Example, you walk into the clothing store and as you do you notice someone quickly coming in your direction, and before you turn in another direction you notice her, or he is wearing an outfit, or has something that is really different, but still classy, like if a she, she has the most beautiful pair of unusual earrings that really stand out.

As she approaches, you notice how 'excited' she seems. She says to you, 'Oh my gosh you are just in time, you've got to come with me and see what we just got in, oh my gosh, just wait when you see the incredible prices. Come on, I'll show you, as she rushes off.

Your curiosity would make you want to follow her. Her excitement and her non boring approach makes you want to see what she has, that has her so excited. She has your full cooperation and your attention. So the point here is, Dare To Be Different. Be Bold. Creative. Original. Exciting. Dazzling and Entertaining. And customers will love it.

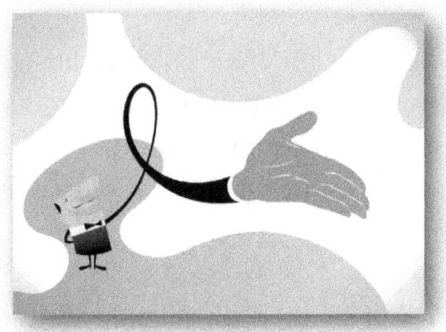

Act 2
The Desk Show

The Dare To Be Different Kind Of Salesperson always does their entire desk show in a way that the customer has never experienced before. Again, this is how to keep the attention of the customer. This 'selling show' is known as a Visual Selling Show.

A Dare To Be Different Salesperson always begins there desk show with the 'logical' reasons the product or service is good for customer. The logical show is probably the hardest part of the show. But it must be done, and done in a way that it applies and registers with the customer and their needs.

It is well known that one of the reasons people do not buy is because they do not understand how it works and how it will benefit them, and that is the reason a Different Kind Of Selling Show is designed to start off with the logic of owning.

As a Dare To Be Different Salesperson, you will design your desk show so everything about the product or service is clearly understood by customer, and they can see everything in words and pictures. Remember the old saying, a picture is worth a thousand words.

The very different kind of salesperson understands that the more a customer can see, along with what they hear, is the reason this different salesperson will always use a 'flip folder' for the logical part of their desk show.

If you use, and you should use a 'visual presentation book', the flip folder is best, because a flip folder only shows one page at a time. Not side by side pages.

The reason you want one that flips up and over, is because if you show two pages side by side, the customers attention will go back and forth between the pages.

Having only one page it is easier to show what you want to stress. By using a flip folder, the customer can only focus on that one page, causing them to focus on that point alone.

The Dare To Be Different Salesperson understands how important it is, that when they are about to make an important point, they mirror their customers body actions. They do this by copying the customer's posture. They talk a bit louder as they lean forward and lightly tense their body before they speak. This is just another way to get customers

A Different Way Of Selling That Dares To Be Different

attention and when you have customers attention, they hear you.

They let the customer see only one page at a time, and in a few short paragraphs they explain about the page, and before flipping that page over, they say, 'any questions.' If there are questions, they answer them and then ask a question that customer would most likely have to answer 'yes' to. They do this each time they flip a page back over.

The reason they keep asking their customers questions that give back a 'yes,' is because, each time the customer answers yes, it helps making it easier for them to say 'yes' at the end.

Also by asking a 'yes' question is that each time they do answer 'yes' the customer is selling themselves. Each 'yes' they give causes them to be convinced that the product or service is good for them.

That is why the Dare To Be Different Salesperson will always ask a question that will get a 'yes' before they move on to the next page. I keep repeating this, as it is one of the most important parts of the Very Different Kind Of Selling Show Presentations.

Now it is very important that before moving on to the benefits of your product or service, that the customer understands fully the 'logical' part before moving on. So it is important to quickly repeat them in short sentences, as you re show your visuals of the logic.

Once the logical flip book show is finished, it is time for the final show before the customer decides if the product or service is logical and if the benefits are worth them purchasing.

Okay, the logical part of owning is over, it's now time to pile on as much sizzle as you can. It's time to really dazzle your customer and this is the fun part of your 'selling show.' You have been building to this with what the customer takes for promises.

Since customers like benefits, now as a Dare To Be Different Salesperson it is now time to put the customer into the show. How? By using the Visual Benefits To Persuade.

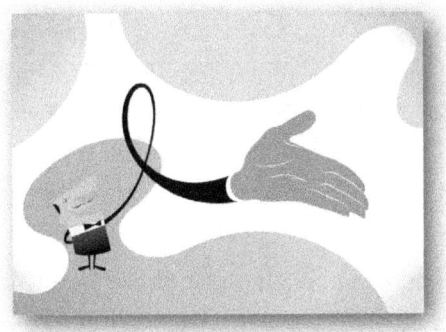

Act 3
Visual Show Of Benefits

Okay, it's time for Act 3 of the 'selling show.' The Benefits. This part of the Different Kind Of Selling is quite important so it necessary that you, the Dare To Be Different Kind Of Salesperson really knows and understands fully the 'benefits' of your product or service as it relates to your customers.

This is where the major need is for customer to be evolved with you, and one way to a customer's help, is by evolving the customer, and the best way to do that is by using visuals.

Visuals that you actually hand to the customer. Remember, each time they take something from you, they are agreeing and are saying yes to you. It is the agreeing you will need when it's time to ask them to purchase.

This is a different visual show from the logical one and it should be a bit jazzy in some way, for attention getting. On the flip visual you customer saw what you were saying, but for the benefits it will be a more hands on show.

So all during the benefits part of the hands on visual show, after customer has been given a verbal benefit in a short paragraph, they are handed a jazzy visual and remember, it is different from the logical one. It is a visual of what they just heard, and this visual helps make the point more true.

The show begins with direct eye contact as your eyes will tell your customers a lot about you. It will tell them if you are totally engaged with them or your just there trying to get through the presentation.

Rapid eye movement and lack of direct eye contact will keep your customers away from trusting in you. Direct fixed eye contact will create trust and proof of interest on your part.

Assuming you have two customers in front of you, for example a husband and wife, most sales people have a tendency to focus on the one customer who is showing most of the interest and actually leaving out the other, but not the Dare To Be Different Salesperson.

After direct eye contact comes a sincere soft smile and with much excitement, customer is told that it is time for the fun part, the benefits, so yes, be excited.

A Different Way Of Selling That Dares To Be Different

Think back to the clothing salesperson who excitedly said, 'Follow me' and how I felt. Well now it's your time to Dare To Be Different and have your customers want to follow you. Follow you to the final 'yes.'

The very different kind of salesperson makes sure this part of the show has all the benefits clearly defined, as they understands a customer does not buy the promises, nor the logical part alone, they also buy the benefits.

What are the benefits? Can the customer see them? Yes, because you are using hands on visuals. The visuals are visual proofs that you have found about your product or service while creating your Very Different Kind Of Selling Show.

Okay, so now it is the time for the cool, Dare To Be Different Kind Of Desk Selling, and for the hands on visual show to begin. The start of the hands on visual show begins with something that has nothing to do with the product or service.

The show begins with the customer being handed something. Something like water, coffee or soda, just anything that they will want to take.

Remember, when customer take something from you, unknown to them, it is a 'yes,' to what is being offered. Once the customer has taken what is being offered, the hands on visual show begins.

The hands on visual show is comprised of 'short points,' followed by a 'visual' backing up what you just said, and it is handed to customer. The visuals are back up proof of what has just been said because customers like to see what you are saying. Customers like proofs. Holding a visual of what they were told will open them up to a 'yes' at the close.

The handed visuals actually show all the benefits of owning the product or service, and are shown one at a time, of what has just been said to the customer. Never give customer more than one visual at a time.

Now an example of using the Different Kind Of Selling Show for a Car Salesperson. A as an example, they could say something like, 'Some customers like the fact that their insurance will be less, or, the gas mileage is so much better. Or the resale. Or anything that can show a benefit of them owning. These are some of the 'benefits' of owning.

So it would be worth the time and effort for this very different kind of car Salesperson to go and find visual things that can be used to hand to customer. You know, like visuals of different reviews of the car they are trying to sell. Or visuals of different insurance prices, or it could be the brochures. Just something to show of what you have stated. Anything that shows a benefit.

After customer has examined the visual, take it back and figure out a way that you can get your customer to re state what you just told them, then once again, asking them if they have any questions.

A Different Way Of Selling That Dares To Be Different

If you should get a 'no,' then ask a question that should get you a 'yes.' If this is done all through the hands on visual persuasion show they will be more likely at the end of the show, when you are ready for a final 'yes' decision, that they will give that final 'yes,' and you have made a sale.

If you cannot create your own far out very different visual shows, hire someone to create one for you. It will be well worth it because buyers bore easily, and that's why it is necessary to entertain them with a totally Different Kind Of Selling Presentation and that is by using visual persuading which acts like proofs.

Again, a Dare To Be Different Kind Of Salesperson presents a benefit with a statement, followed by handing the customer some visual of what they have just said, then ask a question that will get a 'yes' reply.

The hands on visual show will excite customers as the benefits are presented and as you present, you will try say something, anything that will cause the customer to laugh, or at least smile. Again, customers like all people love to laugh and a happy customers makes selling so much easier.

Once you have caused them to laugh they now like you. You make them feel good, and this will make them more likely feel good about owning your product, or service.

Then this Dare To Be Different Kind Of Salesperson will sit back, smile and when the customer thinks there is no more,

95

then as a very different kind of salesperson they will surprise the customer with more verbal benefits followed with yet another visual that's handed to them.

So, no matter what you are selling, no offering, have a hands on visual pertaining to it. Cannot say this too often, after they accept it, you have gotten another yes from them. They just don't know it. Also it is very important that both take from you, if there are two or more people in front of you.

Are you thinking, why is there so much repeating? It is because the more you see or hear the same thing, the more the idea sinks in. Now when customer is even more relaxed, remove the first visual and verbally give them another benefit, and bring out another hands on visual showing that benefit.

To repeat, the more you can get them to take something from you during your desk show will make the taking of your product easier at the end. Also, by them holding the visual, it makes what you have said seem more real to them.

Most important is to always keep your table free of anything other than the visual you are using. After you use a visual, remove it from the table and always put it back in the same place, in case you need to re show it. Then continue the showing of the benefits, using single visuals until you have shown them all and hopefully getting only yes's as you finish with each benefit.

A Different Way Of Selling That Dares To Be Different

If customer knows and understands that you do not want to take from him, but only to exchange with him, they feel better. And again, let the customer know and believe that your first priority is to show them value for their money and then they can decide if it is.

Again, if your inner intent is first about helping your customer get what's best for them and not be thinking about the money, you will get both. All the customer does then, is to exchange his money for your product or service. No winner. No loser. Just an exchange.

No matter how tempting, never sell your customer more than they need. Never sell your customer the higher price item, if the lower meets their need. So loosen up and have fun as you Dare To Be Different with your Different Kind Of Selling Show Presentations.

Ending Of Selling Show

All the logic and all the benefits have been explained and shown, now it is time to ask customer, 'Is there something that you feel our product or service will not be able to do. If there is, what is it.' Wait for the answer, then again, ask a 'yes' question. You will get a yes or you will get a reason. But you should not get a no.

The Dare To Be Different Kind Of Salesperson will tell their customer, now before I get to the bottom line, I want you to know it's no big secret, we want your business, and it's no secret we would like it now.

Also at the end this 'different' salesperson will be sure to make it very clear to the customer that it is their business they want and not just their money. It is told to the customer, 'I use we, because my whole company, not just me wants your business, now and in future needs.'

A Different Way Of Selling That Dares To Be Different

And at the end, the last thing before you ask for the money, is a quick re cap of your Selling Points. Logic, Benefits and Reasons to purchase. Have all your closing points in another unusual looking folder that again, flips back over.

This folder contains visuals from the Logic along with the Benefits at the ending. Do not us all the visuals, but only one or two main from each, Logic, and Benefits

**Hopefully Both You And Your Customers Will Have
Fun During
This Very Different Kind Of Selling**

A Few Recaps

Recap 1

The Gentle Art Of Persuasion

The best form of gentle persuading is by using visuals. They are the most important part of the Different Kind Of Selling Show Presentation.

The Gentle Art of Persuasion

Good persuading starts by relaxing your customer. It's so important and should be the first thing that is done. Tell customer you expect them to be looking out for what's best for them.

The Gentle Art of Persuasion

Asking your customer to be hardnosed and demanding, is also good persuading.

The Gentle Art of Persuasion

Persuasion is being able to influence their future belief. That means that if assumption matches the buyers beliefs they will then accept, and will make a decision to buy.

The Gentle Art of Persuasion

Good persuading is letting the customer know you are on their side.

The Gentle Art of Persuasion

The customer comes in doubting and as long as all you say are wonderful things, their guard will remain up. They need to have all doubts removed or they will spend the time looking for things that are wrong.

The Gentle Art of Persuasion

Persuading is you first stating small negatives, it will now be deleted from the customers mind and they can hopefully give more attention to what your are saying.

The Gentle Art of Persuasion

Gentle persuading is saying things about your product or service in ways that a customer as never heard before. Different words that still speak of what you are offering, again in very different

A Different Way Of Selling That Dares To Be Different

way. That way they are likely to want to listen closer to hear what other thing you may say that they have not heard before.

The Gentle Art of Persuasion

Good persuading is controlling the customers tension and you do this by assuring them, there will be NO pressure at all.

The Gentle Art of Persuasion

As you start to make an important point, us strong gestures, pronounced head movement, and increased facial expressions, along with copying their posture, and speak a little louder and faster as you lean forward and tense your body a little.

This causes the customer to begin paying attention, plus they will have a high level of interest, but most important they will want to see else you may do, as they have not ever seen a salesperson do this, and they do find it interesting and they like that your are different.

The Gentle Art of Persuasion

Good persuading is when you can change customers attitude from a moderate one to one of total acceptance. Ask customer, if we gave this to you as a gift would you take it and use it? Customer should answer yes. Attitude is now changed.

The Gentle Art of Persuasion

To be able to persuade, it's necessary to understand, no one likes to make a 'yes' decision quickly, and lets the customer know right up front that they will 'not' be asked to make a decision today.

The Gentle Art of Persuasion

Gentle persuading is constantly surprising your customer with ways and means of selling they have never experienced before.

The Gentle Art of Persuasion

One of the best ways of gentle persuading, is laughter. Laughter will cause the customer to like you, and that means they will now have an opened minded.

The Gentle Art of Persuasion

Relaxing a customer instead of them putting up defenses, will help them hear you as you begin the process of making comparisons to what they currently have or do, and what you are offering.

The Gentle Art of Persuasion

Persuading is to instantly let the customer he does 'not' have to make a decision today.

A Different Way Of Selling That Dares To Be Different

The Gentle Art of Persuasion

Persuading is using logic, not a boring, long logical presentation, but a short to the point one.

The Gentle Art of Persuasion

Persuading is using proofs that help to establish the truth of something after you say it. A proof is when a statement is made, the visual proof is shown.

The Gentle Art of Persuasion

Your persuasion is attempting to build a preference for changing customers current choice to a much better one for them.

The Gentle Art of Persuasion

Persuading is helping the customer make up his mind about your product or service. You tell your customer that they will be making up their mind whether or not this is better than his current ways.

The Gentle Art of Persuasion

Gentle persuading is letting your customer know it will be them, making a decision, and not you.

The Gentle Art of Persuasion

Good persuading is letting the customer know changes are sometimes frightening and that it's hard for them to give up the known for the unknown. This will let the customer know, this different salesperson knows this is what customer is feeling.

The Gentle Art of Persuasion

Gentle persuading is asking your customer to defer their judgments on what you are selling until the end.

The Gentle Art of Persuasion

Persuading is letting the customer know the reason you will not have to ask them for a decision is because decisions are usually based on comparisons and therefore you will be showing them comparisons, and let them compare what they are doing to what they could be doing.

The Gentle Art of Persuasion

Persuading is asking lots of questions that customer must answer 'yes' to. And each 'yes' answer will guide customer to their final 'yes' at the end.

The Gentle Art of Persuasion

A gentle persuading is changing the intensity of the customer's belief.

A Different Way Of Selling That Dares To Be Different

The Gentle Art of Persuasion.
Persuading is, as you move along in your 'selling show' keep giving customer some kind of a choice in some way. Doing so will be helping to gently persuade them when it is time to make the final decision and it will be on choices not force.

The Gentle Art of Persuasion
To persuade a customer needs continuing assurance all through the selling show, that what they are hearing is what is best for them.

The Gentle Art of Persuasion
Persuading is you being excited to show the customer everything, and let them know why you are in a hurry to show them everything, doing so will create a state of excitement and it will build in your customer at the level of your excitement.

The Gentle Art of Persuasion
Good persuading is also keeping your customer in a state of excitement. Excitement leads to emotions and emotions help lead to a decision. You must keep their emotions excited during the entire 'selling show.'

To keep your customers emotions excited you must push forward the whole time by creating more and more excitement for them. You will have a cancellation if you build on logic alone.

The Gentle Art of Persuasion
Good persuading is free of inconsistencies.

The Gentle Art of Persuasion
Good persuading is always you stating the negatives, thereby eliminating them so your customer can really listen to you. Can't stress how important this is.

The Gentle Art of Persuasion
Persuading is making sure all concealment is avoided. Do not try to hide anything.

The Gentle Art of Persuasion
Great persuading is making sure the buyers point of view has been recognized. And they know it.

The Gentle Art of Persuasion
Great persuading is also knowing that each statement you make should be a statement that forces a customer to think.

The Gentle Art of Persuasion
Right persuading is asking the customer questions that do not inform them, as informing is when you are concerned with

A Different Way Of Selling That Dares To Be Different

the customer understanding the theory, and then you will not be able to sell them.

The Gentle Art of Persuasion

Persuading is speaking very simply and very clearly. Program your selling show so any age can follow it. The simpler the better. And the edgier the better.

The Gentle Art of Persuasion

For good persuading it is important that you use your visual material's in a certain way. You must present them in a way that always shows the customer what you have just said. It reassures the customer.

The Gentle Art of Persuasion

Good persuading is saying things the customer likes to hear, like, 'let's sit back and look at all the facts.' Let's consider them all and see what their importance might be to you.'

The Gentle Art of Persuasion

Gentle persuading is having the customer know you are on their side and will be making sure the product or service is best for them. Your customer feels important that you are taking the time to see what's best for them.

The Gentle Art of Persuasion

The best persuading you can do, is to give a Very Different Kind Of Sales Presentation Show, so that when finished you can sit back and smile, and let your unique Very Different Kind Of Selling stand on its own.

The Gentle Art of Persuasion

Let the customer know, it's their needs and wants and you will be doing your best to fulfill them. They need to know it's not just their money you want. You want their repeated business.

The Gentle Art of Persuasion

A customer needs to know only they will be making their decision based on facts alone. If your inner intent is first about helping your customer get what's best for them and not be thinking about the money, you will get both.

The Gentle Art of Persuasion

Have some kind of 'facts/visuals' to 'show' your customers about the highlights of your product or service.

The Gentle Art of Persuasion

After every statement before moving on to different point, always ask a question that will get a 'yes' answer.

A Different Way Of Selling That Dares To Be Different

The Gentle Art of Persuasion

Never give a long presentation.

This Is How A
DARE TO BE DIFFERENT SALESPERSON
PERSUADES

Recap 2

Questions To Handle

Customer Service
What is Return Policy
How Is Product Different
What Is Gained By Owing
What Are The Benefits For Me
What VALUE Is There For Me
What Real Assurance Do I Have
How USEFUL Will It Be For Me
What If It Doesn't Work as you say
How Can Product Improve My Life
How Will Product Improve My Job
How Is This Product Superior To Others
How Useful Will It Be For My Company
What Are The Benefits For My Company
How Do I Know I Can Trust Your Company
How Can Product Accomplish What I Want

Recap 3

A Dare To Be Different Salesperson Is

Bold
Dazzles
Exciting
Original
Never Lies
Entertaining
Never Prejudges
Never Taken Off Track
Is Always Is Enthusiastic
Always Has A Friendly Smile
Has Back Up Visual Material
Follow-Ups After Every Sale
Only Sell What Customer Needs
Refuses To Become Discouraged
Has Visual Proofs Of What They Say
Can Prove Their Companies Credibility

Barbara Hamilton

Never Gives A Long Presentation Show
Nothing Left Out Of Presentation Show
Develop Faster Ways To Get To The Yes
Creates The Sales Show As To Avoid The No's
Creates Their Own Unique Presentation Shows

Recap 4

A Dare To Be Different Salesperson

Gives Only Needed Information
Never Give Customer All The Information
Repeats Back To Customer Things They Have Said
Knows Repeating Back, Lets Customer Know He Was Listened To
After A Statement He Made Will Ask A Question That Gets A Yes

Recap 5

A Dare To Be Different Salesperson

Makes A List Of All The Benefits
Makes A List Of What Their Promises Are
Makes A List Of Positive And Negative Aspects
Makes A List Of The Reasons Buyer Would Want To Wait
Makes A List Of Reasons Buyer Would Want Think It Over
Makes A List Of Reasons Buyer Would Want To Buy The Product

Are You Willing

Are YOU willing to do all it takes to become a
A DARE TO BE DIFFERENT KIND OF SALESPERSON
BECAUSE
As A
Dare To BeDifferent Kind Of Salesperson

You Will Never Have to Chase The Money - The Sale-

It Will Come To The Dare To Be Different Kind Of Salesperson

Have Fun With The Different Kind Of Selling

www.ingramcontent.com/pod-product-compliance
Lightning Source LLC
Chambersburg PA
CBHW070252230526
45470CB00002B/574